YO POETRY BOOK!

The 99 Best Poems To Feed Your Thirst

By B. Right

Copyright © 2020 by B. Right

All rights reserved. No part of this book may be reproduced or used in any manner without writer permission of the copyright owner except for the use of quotations in a book review.

Numbers for Lunch

Sacred by nature

The numbers don't lie

As I sit down for dinner I order the π

When it arrives I glance at the time

Sequential genius

Aged in my prime

No glasses of wine

Just H20

With green cut of lime

The till receipt number

Chimes 369

Cosmic arrangement

All is in line

The man at the bar

Is a tuned in fellow

Snacking on chips

Made from potato

Conversating with a friend

That he called Haratio

Discussing deeply

The Golden Ratio

Cooking Lesson

You just bought this amazing book

Inside everything is a kloo

Just like a look

Straight to the till

You must took

Babbling knowledge

Just like a brook

Your hand it just shook

Well written and presented

By the most trustworthy crook

In your mind

The words taste cooked

Remember every shepherd

Carries his flook

Channelling

Like Mr Moley

I like to pop up

Pushing through soil

Finally erupt

Tunnel master

Of highest degree

Navigating around

Any root of tree

Plus hangs around

In packs of three

I can also give you a fact for free

It is very beneficial to drink your wee

Enjoy like a fine tea

Plus I can run

Just as fast

In the direction of last

Skates on Kid

Pop the lid

Say hello

To Home-Ed Sid

Two tone Sims hypnotise

N & B bearings

Provide

Quick smooth ride

In these boots I have great pride

To move forward

They must divide

Speed is sharp

Most perfectly timed

Singing along like they've been primed

Set off early

To get to the park

On arrival stands

The almighty vert

My fear of this I must convert

No more living in a yurt

For freefall speed

Has become my need

Follow the Bee

Where he go

We should be

Full of nature

Full of tree

Hear the waters flow

Fast and free

Please navigate

To Terminal 3

Where I'm going

There's no 5G

Farming

The herd is thick

They graze the land

They don't know it

But they have the upper hand

Continue this way

We're heading for sand

Hold out your hand

Let me scan your band

Tie up quick

And give me the grand

Wheat

We – eat

Because the word tells us so

Mass cultivated

GMO

Addicted we are

Time to let go

Fluffy white dough

Has turned into foe

Depleted soils

Have become the last blow

In the future what will we sow

Fake

People Places Stuff

They all crave to be enough

They all pretend

To the bitter end

Online they post and send

Though cause and effect

Will show their defect

Karmic wheel turns

Yet the sun still burns

Smell the ferns

In my forest

You can see

A special tree

When you get there

Bend to your knee

Square Eyes

No TV

Just for a day

Do not worry

You'll be OK

I know you're cluckin for the flicker

Problem is

It just makes you thicker

It can be done

Grab your face

Get off your bum

Go outside

Get involved

And do something

FUN

The Sniper Assassin

Passed down in the DNA

Here to act out

The full play

Like it or not

I own the last say

If you want

I will let you pray

Come round fast

Did the month of May

Sword Fight

818

They resonate

Smashing plate

Sealing fate

Do not be late

Weapon is forged

Tang like the Wu

Vision imprinted

On the paper they drew

Bonding together

Making their crew

I must now reveal

The most obvious clue

The truth is always

Found in you

Masonic Man

What is it you

Can

Do for me

Will your knowledge and rituals

Set me free

Can you take me to

The 33rd degree

Or can I climb the ladder myself

To reach the top shelf

What is up there

Is it a ring

Ding

I just heard a ping

Or was it a humming bird

Voicing her sing

If I am lost can I borrow your thing

You know the compass and square

That you always do bring

Or maybe a grand lodge invitation

For the nation

Sound fair

Chequered floors I hear

Are not so rare

Base level consciousness wouldn't dare

And are you the 5 or 10 percent

Long-term

Is this going to cost us rent

Or is it better

Just to pitch a tent

16

To rhyme in time

Strick with each line

Can be borrowed

From the divine

What's yours

Is mine

Worry no more

For all is fine

Carry on mountain goat

Continue to climb

Hammer Drill

Sat in my van

Slipped disc

Strapped up

Sips from my cup

Turn to Frank

What's up

Lost love for this game

It's no longer the same

Brings in to much pain

Plus there is nothing left to gain

I need a plan

I need to get out

I may have to shout

Ideas flood in

But where to begin

Cash flow is low

I got no bean to sow

But deep within

I feel the know

So I begin to grow

Towards my dream

Though still unseen

I take leaps of faith

For my close team

Greeted with spikes

To cushion my fall

It's a good job I know how to ball

Time will tell

It always does

Hold on

Let go

The landing is clear

For now

I no longer need to fear

For now I see

Process is here

My Kids

Are crazy alive

Hyper buzzing

Like a hive

Always scoping the next ride

They know the game

Because they were born smart

Airborne missiles

Like a dart

Always hitting top of chart

These my blood

They got my heart

Creases of laughter

From just a fart

Family games

The bond is tight

Get to bed

It's nearly midnight

They both swing heavy

In their fight

They are already

Glowing extra bright

For they are gifted

With inner sight

Relevant

Mother earth

What can I write

To give the blind

Much needed sight

Nothing my friend

No more

Can I lend

It's too close to the end

Universal laws have been breached

And a tipping point has been reached

This imbalance cannot last

I may have to fast

Although reconnection is key

Available too for free

Strip the plastic from your feet

And let's re-meet

Grounded my son

To the power of one

Re-tap my heartbeat

In sync with your drum

You know I love you

For I am your mum

Trumpet

Blow it!

Softly

Happy Times

Get on and slide

The ultimate ride

Air off that curb

And continue to glide

Perfect landing to the concrete tide

Hours of youth spent rolling the streets

Amazing all

These people

You meets

Offering exchanges

Of treats and beats

Rubber wheels and quality bearings

Will give you the edge

But only vision and balls

Will take you over the hedge

Liver and Gallbladder Flush

Sat on the throne

Panning for gold

Stuck to the plan

Like I was told

Out they fire

In a gush of bile

Not gonna lie

The smell was vile

Emerald green they shimmer in stink

What do I think

Rinsed and observed

A victorious feeling

Pressure release

Could have hit the ceiling

Bile duct now clear

And the end is near

One more drink of the salty stuff

Wishing to later

When I won't feel so rough

I achieved this

The flow is back on

What can I say

Right on John

Home-School Monkeys

They learn through play

They will always get

What they pretend

Freedom to explore

They will find their own way

Belief and passion

Will drive them through and over

In their pocket

A four leaf clover

They are already a success

In the process

Of passing with flying colours

Their very own test

It's True

The call came when sunk in the bath

Deep meditation

Three hours it last

The message was clear

Though cryptic and blunt

Get this right

No longer the runt

The image had movement

It danced in the flame

Is this classed as insane

A key handed

But where is the lock

Four years I searched

Under every crystal rock

Low and behold

It was just

Writers block

The Original and Best

You press a cure

Four years I invest

Thing is a conscious test

Why won't it let me rest

Hunger to achieve

Just enough to be

Will this be the gig

To finally set me free

New skills new problems

New arena

Though I must push through

Would be a lot easier

To just milk a moo

Pride maybe

Or vision end

Keeps me stuck

Why do I give such a flying fuck

Striving for perfection

To communicate

The message with clarity

It's beginning to mess with my sanity

I even served it on a dish

Problem is

No one really wants fish

It's steak they are after

It's time I moved to better pasture

Roll with the flow

Where does all the cash go

Would love to see the full show

Still people count

And need that help

They even snap and post their painful yelp

But the money machine spins so fast

Which makes it a near impossible task

To jump right in

Need to reprogram

Thoughts from within

A mysterious subject

Which feels dethatched from the divine

Equal spread to me

Would be just fine

The washing load just finished

Better put the wet on the line

A Smile

What power

What presence

What grace

Spread it wide

Across your face

It is like gold

But cannot be sold

It is given when true

To and fro

From me and you

The feeling is shinny

And is all brand new

These a plenty

You must sow

Sunshine

You are my

You did once hurt my eyes

Although now

You make me realise

My true size

Reflecting upon natures prize

Decoding lies

There really is

No compromise

Kobe's Balls

Are big and shinny

Although his brain is pretty tiny

Recall is not his thing

He is more about sniffing bin

They jangle and hang

Paired in wait

For the bang

Like passion fruit with seed

This dog is ready to breed

Just now

A bitch he need

I am Hungry

I know

I am cooking now

It be ready in five

Stop your jive

Help out

Plates in the rack

I can't

I'm busy

I'm making a snack

Scale in Scale out

What's this all about

Look in the stream

To see

Mr brown trout

Look up close

And see how he pout

Then see the moon

From your open room

Test your eyes

And adjust their zoom

Your mind just went boom

Un-weaving the loom

They stepped foot on it

They did

Be careful though

Better not

Blow the lid

Your Mudjesty

Brown

Yellow

Red

You are the original bed

Things that grow you fed

Absorbing intergalactic sound

Forming together

To make a mound

In the beginning

You cost no pound

The Village Down Stream

Is not so clean

A knock on effect

From those living the dream

Eyes glazed

Gut full of cream

What's happened to the serene

Guess what guys

We're all in a team

Can you not hear

The white rabbit scream

Now

One

It all comes back

Do the mathematics

Get back on track

From your job

Just get the sack

That's it

You got the knack

Travel light

Nothing to pack

Lick the tree

Taste the sap

Enjoy the moment

Before you nap

Foxy

You are my oldest friend

That you

Never pretend

Always there to defend

Years gone

Always return

Even when you were sent to burn

No dust in your urn

You've waited long enough

Now it's your turn

Lego Warrior

Forged in a mould

20 million stories

Still untold

You will live

To be very old

Collecting no mould

Always bold

Keep an eye out

Watch him unfold

Trail Of Ink

On the wing of a Condor

Pan pipes be rinsin

Herbal tea

Add me some Ginseng

Acoustic no synth

High in the Andes

Capped with snow

From higher up it's easier to know

Exceptional seats

To the performing show

Machu Picchu

From a tree did grow

Call of the

Wild

My inner child

Far from mild

School me

They tried

Soul almost died

Brain almost fried

Prospects they lied

Always remember

Nature don't hide

Its ticket

To ride

Escape from the city

And seek your new bride

Mountains

Are forged

Through time and pressure

Scale sometimes

Is hard to measure

They bring the curious

Ultimate pleasure

Spend time in them

And you'll find their treasure

VI Kings

As I look out

I begin to see in

Icicles hang long

From Norse bearded chin

Long wooden boat

Is what I came in

Carved not moulded

From lava and tin

Followed the shark

Right behind fin

Then struck land

On sand

And off loaded the band

To instantly disarm

The pretending hand

Let battle commence

The blood is immense

There is no longer pretence

Victory is ours

In reign

And in showers

Bringing forth ultimate powers

Then match to flame

To burn the towers

Then stride toward

And be seated in chair

Flicking golden hair

Once again

Pay homage

To the rightful heir

Touch IT

Amongst the books

There lies a device

Made in the country

Where they grow rice

Pad for eye

At a hefty price

How did the saying go

Three blind mice

Toilet Paper

What's the media bin feedin ya

Stuffin it down your throat

Circling you like a moat

Shield yourself with that special coat

Remember though

That you can float

Seek only the knowledge

That the true has wrote

From the trusted who spoke

Spinning rims

Thou must not poke

Rappers D

If I was an MC

I'd be enzyme Mike

Breaking it down

To AMP up the hype

Spitting lyrics

Right through the pipe

Fruits be dropping

Way before ripe

Powerful messages

To make you enlight

Punch so hard

Bowl win

Any fight

An Elephant

Clay they say

Remembers the day

When nature was misguided

To go the wrong way

Snake like trick

To finger it prick

The anti-venom

Genius

A simple lick

Jah

Time Fire and Fuel

Master to bend any rule

They used to ridicule

Now they lie in a pool

No longer used as a tool

For sight is no fool

Slash now the chains

From my trusty old mule

The Telescope

Brings in great hope

That far away

We can now see

A feeling of glee

Light source connected

With invisible rope

Under strain it will always cope

Hydrus and Indus

Bring wishes they say

That time

Most certainly

Will bring me another day

Brought to me

On a glistening tray

Delivered by wolf

Dragging their sleigh

Red Spy

The spider caught my eye today

Small in size

Big in presence

Master of the room

Poised still and ready

Then made his move

Across my pad

Then a thought

I had

What world so big and different to mine

Could I inherit his skill to climb

Or maybe to weave

Put these together

Image what I'd achieve

And what could I catch

The bigger the net

I'd set the match

Lay eggs too

And watch them hatch

Ignition

Pages turn

People burn

Still no one learn

Up in smoke

Land in urn

Set to wind

Freedom is yearned

Carbon based

There is always a trace

Hats off to the human race

They've finally found their resting place

Tolle

Wake up and witness

With your three eyes

The un-denying prize

The present moment

To everyone's surprise

No longer in disguise

Past and future

Say your goodbyes

This bitch is going to rise

Anchored no more

Releasing all ties

Greta

The big change is coming

I can hear all the drumming

Even some humming

Imprinted on the very large pack

Glow ball events are starting to stack

Let's take it back

To when it was black

Mass memory loss

Got hit in Iraq

Something like

Return of the Mack

Wait my name is Zack

Whoosh

Full swing with a whack

The Motion In The

Dipped my toes in today

The vast beauty they say

Waves they neigh

Fully stretching out

A blanket over unseen ground

Forever moving

From where it has been found

From ripples to death crushing curls

In the right place

You can uncover some pearls

What creature

Lies and lives beneath

Who knows how deep

Remote viewing

Will help me peep

Occasionally you may see

A floating sheep

But never Bo-Peep

Mexican Beer

Your dog is barking

You don't catch no virus

Not in that way

Just Exosomes on the move

This is fearful projection

Sent to divide us

Long played game

Get off the bus

Hysterical masses

They're like a ball of puss

How long can they keep it hush

Supermarkets they gather and rush

If you're from Brizzle

Stay Gert Lush

The Lamb

Is fearless

Born into sunshine

Luscious fresh air

Sticky green grass

Freedom and joy

He has his own pass

A spring in his step

And a zest for life

But Carries no knife

Protection his bleat

And is light on his feet

Plus has many to greet

When hunger sets in

Goes back to the teat

Home Again

As I gently

Take the keys to your house

You look to the floor

And see the brown mouse

He's lived there for years

With the trusty woodlouse

A formidable team

As if they were spouse

They navigate the halls

Naturally rent free

Always seeking

Given opportunity

One favours Brie

And the other rotten tree

NEBula

I know of a clock

That many come to flock

Sits near a dock

And made of rock

This may come

As a shock

But it's easy to unlock

Simply

One turn tick

And one turn tock

On the Tools

Work place bullies

Two I remember

Boxers by trade

Blocks they laid

Walls they spayed

Always got paid

Thought they had it made

Took advantage of their post

Sent fear through most

Went boo like ghost

Tested me over lunch

Pressing their punch

Messed with my meal

They just sealed a deal

Made this shit real

Blood be boiling

So ignorant

Gonna knock off their hats

Hang um like bats

The elder is larger

The leader and barger

After some words were exchanged

He scoped my vision

On steps he stood

To get him higher

Along came me

With extinguisher

For fire

Carbon dioxide

Sprayed to the face

Time quickly progressed

Picked up the pace

Weight be swinging

Anger be flinging

Crowd be singing

I was grappled to the floor

Pinned downward more

Struck from the back

Head felt sore

Still conscious

But feeling wiped

Time to reach for the pipe

Metal held tight

Let's end this fight

Bodies came squawking

Everybody now talking

Stopping me from walking

Then it all gets diffused

And all are confused

Head feeling bruised

Power is now shifted

Held and fused

Bullies bemused

Subconscious lessons were learnt

Respect also earnt

Friendships burnt

Just my way of dealing

To cope with that feeling

Now older and wiser

I can see the geyser

Explosion not needed

For ego not feeded

Eating

What am I supposed to eat

When all I want is a treat

For my ailments to beat

Is it Vegan Raw or Meat

Will Paleo make me soar

What's best to pass my jaw

Where and what is the gluten

Maybe I'll eat more of the fruit'n

Don't tut

But I've lost my nut

I'm stuck in a rut

Processing my gut

Bring on more greens

But not with those beans

What end to what means

Shall I forage or hunt

This diet guy is a…

Micro Squidgy

As I stand

At Williams gates

Lap top under arm

A pen my best mate

Soft and small

Is their operate

Push their buzzer

Bring forward fate

Intercom says

You're never too late

Come dine with us

Grab yourself a plate

Though I never fall for hookless bait

Into the belly I go

To take down this show

Pocket full of glow

Count down to blow

Because now they all know

There's Light at the End

Anxiety and Depression

Is a potent cocktail

Life's pressures wore me down

Heavy became my frown

Pushed me up against the rail

Down come the bars

Now stuck in jail

No chance of bail

Potential life sentence

No liberties or mail

I don't want to fail

My loved ones

Their tale

I feel blind with no brail

I've lost my laugh

Then the years pass

Can't find the green grass

Just a gloomy grey mass

But then I find the Holy Grail

Hope from within

My inner sight

My inner wisdom

Observing my mind

Observing my body

There really is light

I feel like I'm back on track

Less time living in black

Learning to seek

And appreciate

My positivity sack

Buzzy Buzz

Ionization for the nation

Served up cold

Fair play to the bold

Daring not what their told

Knowing that story

Is becoming old

How will it unfold

My blood is gold

Hope we must hold

As it continues

To spread and unroll

Wheelie Bins

They're full of shite

Their contents

Disappears into the night

Kept out sight

Tied up tight

We keep stacking it

But where is it piled

Natures got it dialled

No refuse collection here

No struggle or fight

She's a recycling genius

Always keeping it light

Two Black Cats

The matrix is glitchin

Can't stop thoughts

From pumping and itchin

The other half is witchin

Get out the kitchen

It's time for some switchin

Body be twithin

Agents be snitchin

New program be pitchin

I Have NOTHING

In my loft

It took years

To get to this stage

Now 38 years of age

Just stuff that put me in a cage

Hard work and focus

To get me on this page

In my own garden

I grow purple sage

Herbal books tell me

It's worth spending wage

Numbers Be Poppin

Synchronicities be droppin

Elephants be hoppin

Charts be toppin

Lungs be coffin

There is a new boffin

Car

My whip

My ride

My four wheeled pride

The Silver Bullet

The Wasp

My A to B's

Cost less than one G's

Windows always down

Gotta get the breeze

Famous for saying

Where's my fuckin keys

They represent chapters

And markings in time

First one I had

Was year 99

SR and black

Crashed off the track

Nova by hatch

Sporty by catch

Mr A and Ω

Is in a club

But he's not allowed to blub

For he doesn't want to loose

The bubbles in the tub

And the regular back rub

From the oriental cub

Curtains now dropping

Right down deep

To the midnight sub

Internet going crazy

Better smash up the hub

Organic

When I pick my apple stickers

I choose mine with the nine

She's a bit less guilty

Committed no crime

Sprayed with less slime

Not causing body grime

Not stopping nature's time

Healthy be looking fine

Man of Straw

Through opening he tore

Nothing he wore

Covered in gore

Put straight to the floor

A birth mark he wore

Pounds and ounces

Then the established pounces

Register the child

Sounds very mild

Profile stockpiled

Value to compile

By the Tick and the Tile

Name now on file

Go swim up the Nile

Merry Go

At the centre

There lies your truth

Step inside

The circular booth

Run by red Ruth

Step outside

And start to slide

Not a nice ride

Knowing that circles

Always love two divide

A.I

In the beginning

It was slow

Not much did it know

On off

Was its main flow

If dropped on toe

Your temper would blow

But now we bring it

Wherever we go

Flaunting it to friends

Always wanting to show

It listens to us

But has it a heart

Can it see beauty

In the thing we call art

Always leading us back to cart

Its beats are hypnotic

Puts minds in a trance

It's a dangerous dance

But still we enhance

Front and Back Eyes

It's hard to cover both doors

On multiple floors

Anxiety soars

Sweat leaks from pores

In the distance

I hear roars

I need my 360 vision

To tune in all senses

My tornado spins

And destroys all fences

Including pretences

Returning back to the centre

Where nothing can enter

Tiger

It's orange

It's black

No pressure

On its back

Always focused

Always on track

Courage it does not lack

Knows how to hack

Picks up the slack

Pay attention

For its slash

Will now whack

Downlock Chillin

As I lie

Under the Beech

Crispy leaves

Two bare feet

Who do I meet

Mr rude did not greet

Zombie dog

With funny beak

Conversation got neat

Felt some heat

Another one scared

Of the big boo Pete

Weaving Spiders

Come not here

Echo's a cheer

Sit next to the lake

And enjoy the sips

From your German beers

Let the hot tub and music

Soothe all of your fears

Laugh and chuckle

With your aging peers

If they fall from your face

They're just called tears

It's Easy

Repeat after me

My MIND is FREE

Go hug a tree

All eyes now open

And able to see

A feeling of glee

Unlimited freedom

To simply just be

Sip back your tea

And notice the beauty

Your big family tree

Flatty

I found a new map

It was left in a trap

But it fell to my lap

Different to most

Unveiling new coast

With perimeter of ice

No trees just weiss

So I flew there by nap

And opened the tap

There I met

A bloody nice chap

Who calmly explained

All of the crap

Told of the future

UFO's from the skies

They will zap

Zippy

2 years old

He's due another

And I'm not feeling that fab

Anxious feelings flood my gut

Discussion of options

Ends in a rut

So off we head to the clinical hut

Invisible ingredients

Expected to trust

Read all the info

Tells us

That we must

The following days

My eagle eye tracks

Seams in a haze

And a change in health

Eyes fall back

Starts to shake

This is no longer fake

Not sure what to make

But all is ok

Is what they say

But I swear right now

He's different

To other day

So I begin to pray

Nervous energy

Leads to sleepless nights

From health to unsure

I wish for a cure

My heart does now pour

Can't wait for the next one

When he's aged 4

Periodic

Around my table

There sits some big hitters

Never does fear

Give them the jitters

Some professional in the art of

Tweaking twitters

Raised with no sitters

Mind

They just lit hers

Crumbs

Under the breadline

Is flippin tough

It's not even like

You even want stuff

Just crave to have enough

So things aren't so rough

Acting is exhausting

When will they call your bluff

Please god

Release these cuffs

Mr Banks is bleedin me dry

No matter how hard I try

Did the one man car boot

You laugh

But no lie

The Big Bang

Dance like Stephen Hawking

Let your robot do the talking

Split the dancefloor

The club be squawking

Moves be walking

Politics be forking

Snort two Tequilas

Make some room

For Richard Dawkins

Bubbling Emotions

Words on page

Scent in the burner

Preferably Sage

Easy sometimes

To be consumed by rage

Whatever you do

Don't rattle the cage

Emotional intelligence

Will surely come with age

When you put the work in

It will most certainly pay

Foxglove

Are you not fed up

With doing what your told

Is this practice

Growing rapidly old

When was soul

Advertised and sold

For paper and gold

You must regain hold

Pushing through the damp

And the cold

Remaining brave and bold

Then witness the beauty

Truly unfold

Herb

Clear communication

Like a DK book

So you all get the hook

Message delivered

By an authentic rook

In the game of chess

It's the one

That took

Dot to Dot

Will reveal the plot

Keep it going

Untill you got

Loosen the lid

Look in the pot

Knowledge that's hot

Three big dogs

Went down that day

Deep in the iceberg town

Mouths do say

In the twilight they lay

For air they did pray

The waves did neigh

Yes they all passed

But one came back

Through death and black

Via wormhole and crack

Armed with the sack

He walks the land today

And he's about to collect

His much owed pay

Alan

Is a TV believer

Illusion receiver

Gossip breeder

Nonsense feeder

Comfort needer

Plays follow the leader

Time to

Wake up your reader

Propagate your seeder

Take back the root

Get on some boot

And give your horn

A bloody good hoot

The Stars Say

I'm a Pisces

So I guess

I should go jump in the bath

Plus go live in the sea

Amongst all the floating plastic

And highly toxic debris

Most of my friends will be scaly

Shoal school they will attend daily

Never do they blink

In the deep blue sink

Though something is rising

Mercury the icing

Something dyer

A good friend of mine

Is off to the fryer

A potential buyer

To the chippy in Clapham

Where the guy cooks um fast

And knows how to wrap um

Enema

Chug that bag

Down in one

No pause no drag

2 litres shoot down

The pipe and the lag

Colon at the ready

Hold fast and steady

Need to relax

Where's my teddy

Led back on the rug

Now feeling snug

Coconut oil

Makes for super smooth plug

Essential cleansing

Removing toxins

And evil stomach bugs

Time to give tummy

Some much needed love

Then I glance to the clock

It looks back and it mocks

6 minutes in

Noisy with its tocks

Committed now

Must hold to the end

First few are challenging

This is no pretend

Need to make 20 deep

Benefits I will reap

Rewards to keep

But I'm starting to seep

12 minutes now

Somethings gotta give

Water wants to live

Sometimes a sieve

Time for pressure release

Aimed into china piece

Then a smirk does crease

All is at peace

Foot Ears

I've started listening

Through the soles of my feet

When it rains

They sink firmly

Back into the peat

Mud between toes

There's an unusual fast beat

Up in the trees

The Tits go tweet

To each other they greet

Electrons discharge

Through vibrations and heat

It's OK

To let me lead

I found the seed

Don't roll back

Towards the crack

That empty void

Where knowledge is lack

Dangerous and vast

Is this trap

Stay alert

No time to nap

Quick go check

The vitals sack

Comfort the young

And family on lap

The hiding one

Has released the tap

The Devil is a Pussy CAT

I've seen her claws

Confusing laws

Unhardened paws

Weak slack jaws

Has not the ability

To press stop/pause

Plays the same moves

It's beginning to bore

Clues I'm finding

All over my floor

Sweat is leaking

And is starting to pour

Wound getting sore

News flash to pussy CAT

You forgot the front door

Crystals Keep Time

Most end in ite

They come awake

In the twinkling of night

Aiding mediation and much given sight

Compounds are tight

Polished some bright

Collecting information by light

Tune in correctly

Fly high like a kite

To a serious height

But harbour no fright

Piezoelectric

Press um just might

Savanna

Lions hunt at night

For darkness brings

The opportunity

Strong is the pride

13 deep

Full moon

Allows them to peep

Nutrition they seek

Stealthy they creep

Far from any jeep

Respecting the laws of the land

From grass to sand

Tight is this band

Mess with them

They'll bite of your hand

Germ THEORY

It did spread

But now

Is dead

ClO2

Chemistry for the people

Oxidiser for the blood

Shout high

From the steeple

So simple sometimes

A solution at hand

Come join the band

Who health

Want to land

Who and What?

Is the Governing Mentality

Pitching and presenting

Our given reality

To all of humanity

Questions to pose

Are pressure and gravity

Feel Good Now

You got the POW!

FRYing up Poems

Like Mr Stephen

Mixing up odds

With remarkable evens

Please enter

The mosh pit

With 23 Heathens

Poetry is Primal

It needs a revival

For our future

And survival

A spiritual adventure

Cracking through denture

Gets straight to the point

Like a super strong joint

Instant Medicine

For all of the mind

For all of Mankind

Portrait

Go look in the mirror

See the light in your eyes

Un-glaze and re-shimmer

Turn up the dimmer

Pupils dilate

You're never too late

To meet and greet

Your reflective mate

Looking so good

Go hang in the Tate

Your Mantra

Happy Healthy and Free

Repeat after me

Unlock inner Chi

Allowing one

To simply just be

Windy Ears

A walk in the wind

Can help clear the mind

For there's nothing to find

Help to leave things behind

For this nature is kind

And perfectly timed

There's no hills to climb

Easy on limbs

Codons do chime

Living Your Dreams

Is easy it seams

For those

Rolling reams

Of laughter

And gleams

They have their own teams

Stacked magic beans

It keeps growing better

They just add some wetter

They know the secret letter

Energy tapping

Quick running like go getters

Gun dogs

They got three Setters

Four Poems in ONE

Downloaded from the sun

Till kingdom come

Nowhere to run

Listen to the hum

Sailors grab for Rum

Air there is now none

For it is done

Breathing now

Not so fun

Crashing rocks

Press a tonne

But there is hope

In the distance

I heard it from my son

Flaming Mathematics

Reducing all to ONE

Thank you for reading my poems

Hopefully they will have sparked something within you

If you have enjoyed please leave a review

More poems I'll continue to write just for you

About the Author

I woke one morning and decided to write. I am passionate about living in tune with nature and living a healthy and simple life. Always inquisitive and forever hungry to learn.

Printed in Great Britain
by Amazon